CN00872228

A Field Guide To Continuous Delivery

by Made Tech

ISBN: 1530121418

First Printing: February 2016

www.madetech.com

Introduction

As a team who practice Continuous Delivery and have extensive experience in introducing it to numerous organisations, we've had quite a lot to say on the subject.

This book is a collection of ten essays written by the Made Tech team, previously published at www.madetech.com/blog, with each one discussing a different facet of Continuous Delivery.

Over the course of reading this book, you'll learn how Continuous Delivery can benefit you, what it means to practice it, the tools and mindsets you'll need to adopt, and the challenges you may face in the transition to a more efficient, painless workflow.

Chapter 1: What is Continuous Delivery?

by Scott Mason

In today's world of instant communication, businesses need to be able to move quickly to meet the ever changing needs of their customers, especially so when it comes to building, maintaining and evolving the online platforms of those businesses.

Past development practices didn't always lend themselves to this fact, with releases taking place weeks or even months apart, and huge change sets being the norm.

At its inception, the goal of Continuous Delivery was to find a way to optimise those practices to the point where small, iterative releases could happen, leading to releases that are safely deployable to a production environment at any time, and are deployed as often as several times a day.

For businesses, this is incredibly valuable, in that they are then able to get features to, and feedback from, their customers at a much faster rate. For developers, they can be confident that what used to be a very painful process is now simple, mundane even, and that the code they release is stable.

Where did Continuous Delivery come from?

In a nutshell, Continuous Delivery was borne, many eons ago (i.e. within the last twenty years), out of the frustration of developers stuck in what was known as 'Integration Hell', the point at which the code you've been working on for the last few weeks meets the code that the rest of your team has been working on in that period, and the point at which you realise those two code bases are incompatible in subtle and sometimes devastating ways.

It used to be that a project would be worked on by a team of developers who each went away to work on their own area of code for periods of weeks or even months at a time, after which all of the work would be brought together, and everyone would knowingly walk into Integration Hell. Developers are problem solvers by nature and, as a huge pain point, this was a problem that very much needed to be solved.

Automation for the people

One such solution was Steve McConnell's 'Daily Build and Smoke Test'[1], from 1996. His idea was for all code to be tested at the end of every day and run as a 'smoke test', an automated process that immediately 'broke the build' should it find any fundamental problems.

His reasoning was that if anything did break, chances were that it would be much simpler to fix something that had cropped up in the last 24 hours than it would be to fix something that had occurred at some point within the last month.

The idea struck a chord, and later, over at Thoughtworks, Matt Foemmel, along with Martin Fowler, took a similar concept introduced by the Extreme Programming methodology and developed it into something much bigger. This concept was called Continuous Integration (not to be confused with Continuous Delivery).

The pair wrote about their experiences in a popular article[2], the broad strokes being that developers should be contributing code to a single repository under source control, which then, automatically, runs a series of tests, followed by a build on success.

While the build and testing steps are automated, there is still (and most likely always will be) a necessarily manual step to all of this, in that individual developers are themselves responsible for reintegrating several times a day.

Integration problems will still occasionally arise, it just means that when they do occur, they occur early, and are usually small enough to prevent another trip into Integration Hell, making the entire process demonstrably less painful for everyone.

As an added bonus, the fact that all of the code is committed to a single repository means that new developers can join the project without needing to spend days setting up a development environment, again increasing the speed at which a project can move.

So, what is Continuous Delivery?

Where Continuous Integration is about making it easier for multiple developers to work on the same project together, Continuous Delivery is about how we make it easy to get that work quickly and safely to production, and out into the wild, actually delivering value to Product Owners and their users.

This transition from development to production is facilitated by what's known as a build pipeline, which houses a number of different 'environments'. The pipeline handles the process of advancing our code through each of these environments, whereby upon a successful build in a given environment (which includes our automated tests), we are then able to trigger a build in the next environment, either automatically or manually.

Each environment serves a different purpose, and different development teams will create pipelines with any number of environments to meet their needs. What's important is that the pipeline is set up in such a way that developers can road test their code in a production-like environment, with production-like data, and that new features can be previewed and tested by the Product Owner. The ultimate destination for our code is, of course, the production environment.

What Continuous Delivery is, then, is the ability to push that code through the build pipeline all the way to production, with confidence, at a moment's notice. While the Product Owner may not want those new features to go live just yet, by getting the code successfully all the way through to the staging environment and having both you and the Product Owner review it, you can be sure that when you are given the go ahead, the push to production will be a painless one.

---

[1] http://www.stevemcconnell.com/ieeesoftware/bp04.htm

[2] http://www.martinfowler.com/articles/ originalContinuousIntegration.html

Chapter 2: The Benefits of Continuous Delivery

by Chris Blackburn

Continuous Delivery is a technique that grew roots in the IT department, but is very much focused on delivering value, in the shape of shipped software, back to the business more frequently and more reliably.

Most modern software companies focus on delivering Software as a Service over the Internet, and while they maybe able to realise many of these benefits if they're delivering software via another mechanism such as application installs, there may be some areas where they're less able to move at an 'as a Service pace'.

There are a number of reasons why organisations who take software delivery seriously should be investing in Continuous Delivery.

Faster to market

The primary business drivers behind Continuous Delivery adoption are that it both facilitates and encourages shorter delivery cycles.

Continuous Delivery practitioners must be integrating their work with the rest of the team at least once per day, and ideally, a couple of times an hour.

This can encourage stakeholders across the organisation to start thinking of software delivery as a series of smaller features. The demands of keeping a single software product release-ready, without making use of patterns such as feature branching, are made trickier when delivering particularly big changes.

By releasing small features more regularly, software and the value that it's intended to deliver gets in to the hands of customers faster. The sooner you can get software to customers, the sooner you can start getting feedback, and the less time you spend working on unnecessary or less valuable features.

As more organisations adopt fast release cycles, this is becoming the norm. Businesses such as Slack, the team communication tool, make much of their "What's New" feature, which highlights the changes that have been released in the past day.

Improved engineering practices

Continuous Delivery has become the catalyst for improving development practices through the delivery cycle, from project inception through to maintenance.

The need to keep software release ready encourages or even, some might say, demands the adoption of good software engineering practices, such as Test-Driven Development, Behaviour-Driven Development, and Pair Programming, techniques that, over the course of a software project, will increase your ability to move quickly with confidence.

When the business demands more regular release cycles, technology teams are incentivised to leverage higher levels of automation. With more regular builds, resource intensive manual QA processes should be replaced in part, or ideally in full, with automated UAT suites. Performance testing and the associated provisioning of infrastructure can be automated, as can security testing.

Reduced risk

Big releases containing many changesets, which in extreme cases may represent the culmination of many months work, offer significant risk. The larger the deployment, the more likely it is that something will go wrong.

By contrast, releasing little and often keeps changesets small, and subsequently, the risk of the change introducing issue is reduced.

In addition, by practising deployments more regularly, we become better at them. We feel the pain of bad deployment practices more regularly, we're better incentivised to replace manual steps with automation, and so the risk associated with human error becomes a less likely occurrence, and releases become a less resource intensive practice.

Where possible, a general principal would be to not be overly scared of acceptable production bugs to the detriment of moving quickly. Where software is released close to it being built, resolving issues is generally made easier as memory of the implementation is fresh. When coupled with a fast, automated pipeline that allows followup fixes to be released quickly, issues can often be squashed before they're even noticed.

Releasing is a business decision

Too often, releasing software updates is a technology-lead decision, rather than a commercial decision.

In many organisations, releasing is a process encumbered with risk and involves a highly orchestrated series of manual steps, each of which offers an opportunity for error. A good Continuous Delivery environment replaces these manual steps with automated tooling.

By encouraging discipline within the team to ensure software is always in a release-ready state, the decision to release new features and updates can be moved back to where it belongs: with the commercial stakeholders.

In particularly mature Continuous Delivery teams, an organisation can go as far as empowering Product Owners to physically push the button to make a release whenever they're happy with the changeset, in a complete absence of operations folk standing by in support.

Beyond this, teams can move a step further to practising Continuous Deployment. In a typical Continuous Delivery setup, full automation usually happens as far as a staging/ pre-production environment, with a manual button-push to trigger the production release. Continuous Deployment fully automates this final step, so that a code check-in that passes all previous steps in the pipeline will be automatically deployed to the production environment.

Exposing inefficiencies

The adoption of Continuous Delivery is a strong tool in exposing inefficiencies through the software delivery process, from insufficient requirement description, to unexplainable change control processes.

By tightening up discipline and tooling around the build and deployment process, and particularly by focusing on delivering incremental release-ready features, the true barriers preventing an organisation from moving fast become blindingly obvious.

In many cases, outdated technology practices can be a strong force in preventing software being delivered in an acceptable or ideal timeframe for an organisation. However, as more businesses realise that they're actually software companies in disguise, there are many factors outside of actually building the software that can hold businesses back. By getting the software delivery process right, an organisation loses the most obvious reason for slow software delivery, allowing it to focus on fixing wider issues.

Chapter 3: Preparing Your Team for Continuous Delivery

by Emile Swarts

It can be challenging to get sufficient infrastructure set up to enable you to practice Continuous Delivery, but the biggest challenge may be changing the way you and your team think about releasing software.

The goal is to evolve software in small increments, not to drastically change it all at once. As the previous chapter has shown, this makes releasing software faster, more reliable and easier to debug. Each contribution or commit has to be releasable, without question.

As unreasonably optimistic as this sounds, it is possible, and people have been doing it for years.

Releasing to production should be boring, boring to the point that there is no need to notify anyone that you are doing so. If someone has a commit in the pipeline that should not be deployed to production without further work, then you are not practicing Continuous Delivery.

If a team member introduces a bad commit, it is their responsibility to fix it. If this starts to block the deployment pipeline, the commit may need to be reverted.

Developers can be reluctant to adopt such a drastic change of pace, but once you begin to see the benefits we've discussed, you and your team will never look back.

To succeed, it is vital for every single member of the team to stick to the following guidelines, in order to successfully practice Continuous Delivery.

The art of sneaking it into production undetected

Production is the one and only source of truth. Something may work in a non-production environment, but that does not necessarily mean that it works in production.

When you work on a feature, aim to get 99% of it deployed into production undetected, by the customers, users, and the rest of the code in the system. This is sometimes known as dark launching, and as you become proficient in Continuous Delivery, you will do more and more of this.

Dark launching can sometimes be something as simple as omitting a hyperlink to a page, other times it is more complex, but it is never impossible. Feature toggles, which we'll discuss in Chapter 7, may be used when dark launching becomes too complicated, but should be treated as a last resort.

By getting your code into production early, it has proved to some degree that it can co-exist with the rest of the system, and that none of the other existing functionality has regressed.

Using this method, you'll find that your definition of "done" shifts from an arbitrary verification in a pre-production environment to actually verifying the code in production, because it has become so easy to do so safely.

Communicate with commit messages

If a developer has not committed all day, there is no way of telling how their work will fit in with the rest of the system. Frequent commits mean that you have considered the bigger picture and that you have broken this down into smaller, more manageable sub-problems.

A positive side-effect of this are commit messages, the notes written to accompany and describe what a given commit achieves. The more well written and descriptive a commit message is, the more useful it is to other members of the team.

By then looking at the commit history of a project, team members get a lot of feedback on the current state of that project.

The commit history will help you quickly discover miscommunications, or people heading in the wrong direction with their intended solutions. In big teams this becomes vital. Merge conflicts become less frequent and less complicated to solve.

It can be easy for developers to lose track of who has committed what and when, so a common practice is to hook up your version control system to your company chat application, so that an announcement is made automatically every time a new commit is pushed to master. This allows everyone to stay up to date on the current state of the project with minimal effort.

Confidence obstacles

Chapter 8 addresses this in more detail, but it's important to have confidence in the decisions you make on how to solve a problem, and that there is nothing blocking your path further down the line.

At times there may be missing or incomplete specifications that, when revealed, will require your system to adapt at a moment's notice.

If this happens often, it may encourage developers not to push small commits often, as it leads to uncertainty over whether their intended solution will ultimately be the correct one.

Practicing good Continuous Delivery means clarifying your intentions with a particular problem before you start writing large amounts code. By committing early and often, as soon as the first commit goes in, everyone is able to feed back on that work, which benefits the overall project.

This also promotes the quality of code, as smaller chunks are easier to analyse by other team members, making it much harder for poor quality code to sneak in undetected.

Production awareness

When developing new features, it is vital to consider how they will ultimately be released to production as soon as you begin working on them. This may mean pulling down a copy of real production data, anonymising it, and verifying the code against it in your development environment.

You should also be testing your feature as much as possible in your staging environment and having your automated tests prove, to a certain degree, that everything is as it should be.

Once you've continued to move your code through the pipeline, having something like a blue/green or a canary release system means there's a production environment in which you can test and verify your code, safe in the knowledge that it's not accessible by the public until you make the final switch.

Finally, when implementing new features, it is often necessary to clean up our database tables and alter schemas, in order to keep our codebase tidy and to remove code that has become irrelevant.

These cleanup tasks should typically be the last step in deploying a new feature, when you can make absolutely certain that no other environment in your pipeline depends on this data.

It's important to develop the foresight never to negatively affect your running production environment.

Big bang deploys are your enemy

Big bang deploys mean releasing a large amount of code into production at a time, and Continuous Delivery means avoiding these like the plague.

Introducing thousands of lines of code into a running system can have unexpected consequences. The sheer volume of code makes it difficult to know exactly what went wrong, and where it went wrong. Worse still is that a large, faulty deploy to production is incredibly difficult to remedy as there's a good chance that you won't easily be able to rollback to an earlier state.

On the other hand, small commits reduce that risk exponentially. Your build pipeline, described in Chapter 5, gives you instant feedback on the quality of your change as soon as it is released. Should something go wrong, you can act on it immediately, and you only have a handful of potential suspects to debug.

Continuous Delivery means having the discipline to stick to these principles even when it is difficult to do so. Your software will be the better for it in the long term.

Chapter 4: Continuous Delivery Tools

by Seb Ashton

Finding the right solution to form the basis of your Continuous Delivery work flow is key, and you really need one that will fit into your existing way of working with minimal effort.

When choosing your platform, be it Software as a Service (SaaS) or self-hosted, you need to be confident that it will offer you and your team a pain free Continuous Delivery workflow.

Factors that can influence this decision will range from the amount of work needed for initial setup, to the time it will take to perform any ongoing maintenance, and finally how easily it will integrate with your current setup.

Essential features

Whilst every SaaS or self-hosted solution on the market boasts numerous feature sets, there are a handful of core features that are essential to operating a successful pipeline.

Integration with version control

Version control integration is the most crucial feature your chosen solution should possess. It should poll your repository, or at least use web hooks to detect changes, which should then initiate a new build and subsequently trigger the rest of your Continuous Delivery pipeline process.

Custom script execution

Custom script execution within a pipeline step is a key feature, particularly if you rely on bespoke build actions.

Thanks to buildpacks, many common deployments are very simple, but often the need arises to run custom deploy scripts. In these instances the ability to use tools like Capistrano[3] to execute deployment tasks is vital. While it is written in Ruby it can be used to deploy almost any project, thanks to the open source community behind it.

A pipeline

Pipelines are discussed in depth in the next chapter, but your solution should provide a pipeline view, a visual representation of all your deployment steps.

Notifications

For software engineers, switching contexts can be really distracting so your Continuous Delivery solution should offer a way to alert your team to any successful or failed deploys without them needing to check a web interface.

This can be as simple as an email, however many Continuous Delivery platforms will also integrate with the popular team chat programs, such as HipChat[4] or Slack[5].

Self-Hosted vs SaaS

A SaaS solution usually requires just a one click install, and something like a YAML file for configuration, whereas a self-hosted solution will require a lot more set up at the outset.

However, the investment in infrastructure, and other set up required with a self-hosted solution, will be recouped over a number of applications, and will allow you more flexibility in the long term, such as being able to implement features provided from community plugins and extensions. You won't find this flexibility in a SaaS solution, where you are tied to their feature set and development cycle of adding new features.

Self-Hosted Options

The following is a selection of solutions that provide said features, which the market currently offers:

Jenkins CI[6]

Whilst technically a Continuous Integration platform, with the addition of the build pipeline plugin it is easily configured to be a complete Continuous Integration and Continuous Delivery solution.

Go[7]

Go is a Continuous Delivery platform written and maintained by the folks at ThoughtWorks, who literally wrote the book on Continuous Delivery. As you can imagine Go is based on a lot of the principles outlined in it. Like Jenkins (with the build pipeline plugins) it will perform both Continuous Integration and Continuous Delivery.

Spinnaker[8]

As the newest option on the list, Spinnaker differs from the previous two by virtue of being purely a Continuous Delivery platform. Spinnaker will take a deployable asset, such as a Docker image, and deploy it out though the pipeline steps, but only once it has received trigger from a separate CI platform like Jenkins.

SaaS Options

Cloudbees[9]

Cloudbees is Jenkins in the cloud. Cloudbees uses a Workflow plugin, which you could implement on your self-hosted Jenkins instance, to add Continuous Delivery functionality.

If you like the services provided by the self-hosted Jenkins, but no longer want to maintain the infrastructure, then this could be an option for you.

Snap CI[10]

Snap, like many SaaS offerings, is tied to GitHub, at least at the time of writing. Snap enables you to build both simple linear pipelines, and advanced branched pipelines from a single, or even multiple, repositories.

Harrow IO[11]

Harrow IO is a SaaS solution from the folks who maintain Capistrano. Whilst you can use any script to run your integration and delivery steps, Harrow provides simple integration if you are already using Capistrano scripts to execute deployments.

Options for both SaaS and self-hosted solutions are always emerging and evolving, and different teams have very different requirements, so it's important to do your own research and find out which best suits your Continuous Delivery workflow.

A good rule of thumb, however, is if you're maintaining a single product, a SaaS solution will most likely be what you need, as you wont have to worry about the additional infrastructure. On the other hand, if you deliver a large number client of projects, a self-hosted solution that can be tailored to your needs will ultimately be a better fit.

-----

3 http://capistranorb.com/

4 https://www.hipchat.com/

5 https://slack.com/

6 https://jenkins-ci.org/

7 https://www.go.cd/

8 https://github.com/spinnaker/spinnaker

9 https://www.cloudbees.com

10 https://snap-ci.com/

11 https://www.harrow.io/

Chapter 5: Building a Pipeline

by David Winter

A pipeline is a set of steps that your code takes to get from a developer's local machine through to a production environment. This pipeline is managed by a tool (see Chapter 4 for examples) which lets you define these steps, what they do, and how and when it proceeds onto the next one.

Which steps in the pipeline you create is completely dependent on the application you want to deliver, and any processes you might have to get it verified and into a production state.

Continuous Delivery Pipeline

Common pipeline steps

Most commonly, the first step focuses on Continuous Integration. All developers are pushing into a central code repository and committing early and often. The pipeline will then run your automated test suites to make sure new code doesn't break. If any tests fail, that code goes no further through the pipeline until it's fixed.

Once you have a reliable build, steps that follow in the pipeline can involve deployments to various staging environments where your team, and perhaps your product owner, can preview the code changes.

At the end of the pipeline is always your end product. Either a production deploy, or release of your application that is ready to be released to the end audience.

As an example, we'll use a pipeline structure consisting of the following steps:

1. Build
2. Continuous
3. Staging
4. Production
5. Production flip (for Blue/Green deployments)

Let's now talk about how we progress a new set of code changes through a pipeline.

Triggers

Each step in your pipeline needs to be initiated by some means. These can be manual or automatic triggers.

New builds through your pipeline should be triggered automatically when new code is pushed into your central code repository. This involves either periodic polling of the repository by your tool, or push notifications from the repository. Either of which will trigger a new build. This gets the ball rolling.

Subsequent steps are then triggered automatically as each previous step succeeds, until a point is reached where human verification of your application is required for it to progress further through the pipeline. This may be to visually check a UI or UX change, or it may be that a Product Owner needs to sign off on a new feature before it is released.

If your pipeline consists of nothing but automated steps, then you're practising Continuous Deployment too.

Repository representation of the pipeline

With branches and tags in your source code control, you can easily mirror the state of your pipeline in your repository. Each of your pipeline steps can be configured to push the code into a branch with a name matching that of the current step if it succeeds, with the following step pulling from that branch.

When a build is triggered for a pipeline it's given a number. Making use of this number as a repository tag gives you good historical references, and makes browsing different releases easier in tools such as GitHub. Also, if you have a bug for a previous release, you can easily checkout based on a tag name (or branch) rather than trying to find a specific commit based on a date.

Build step commands

Besides a step leading to another step, how do we get them to actually do something, like running tests, or deploying code?

All tools come with a mechanism to execute an action or actions for a particular step. Depending on which you're using, it might be an integration with another online service, or one that allows you to specify custom commands. These give you the most flexibility if your needs are more complex.

You could list the various commands that your step requires to complete, one after the other in the pipeline tool configuration. However, it's good practice to use a shell script, as it allows you to group those multiple commands into one, and to keep the script in your repository.

Be descriptive with the names of your shell scripts. Have a step that needs to run tests? Why not have a script called pipeline/tests. Performance? pipeline/performance. Your pipeline tool then only needs to know of one command to run per step, and you've got all the benefits of source code control for your pipeline logic, as well as the ability to run these commands locally.

It's worth noting that there might be limitations with what you execute at each step. If you have a self hosted tool, such as Jenkins, you need to ensure any dependencies your scripts have are on the system Jenkins is running on.

As an example, if you're using RSpec for tests, your system would need Ruby, RubyGems and RSpec installed. If you're using a hosted tool, then build steps are usually run within virtual containers, and often the services allow you to install any of your step dependencies before they are run, or they have common virtual containers already that you can specify. So, there might be a Ruby container that would already have most common dependencies in place.

Breaking down our pipeline

Lets go into a bit more detail with our example pipeline. For each of the steps, we'll talk about the trigger, how it's linked to our repository, what it executes and what step happens afterwards.

Build
- **Purpose:** To ensure the latest code passes our tests and code standards
- **Trigger:** Automatic, by someone committing to the master branch of our repository.
- **Pulls from branch:** master
- **Executes:** pipeline/tests, pipeline/code-standards

- **Success push branch:** build
- **On success:** Trigger the continuous step to run automatically

Continuous

- **Purpose:** To deploy the code to a staging area for the development team to preview and check that all the code our developers have integrated works as expected.
- **Trigger:** Automatic, on success of the previous build step
- **Pulls from branch:** build
- **Executes:** pipeline/deploy/continuous
- **Success push branch:** continuous
- **On success:** Create a manual trigger for the staging step as the next in the pipeline

Staging

- **Purpose:** To deploy code to a staging area for a client to preview.
- **Trigger:** Manual, if the development team are happy with the continuous deploy
- **Pulls from branch:** continuous
- **Executes:** pipeline/deploy/staging
- **Success push branch:** staging
- **On success:** Create a manual trigger for the production step as the next in the pipeline

Production

- **Purpose:** To deploy to the production environment when the client is satisfied with the staging deploy.
- **Trigger:** Manual, if the client is happy with the staging deploy

- **Pulls from branch:** staging
- **Executes:** pipeline/deploy/production
- **Success push branch:** production
- **On success:** Create a manual trigger for the production-flip step as the next in the pipeline

Production flip

- **Purpose:** After a final verification in a non-public production environment, flip live traffic to the new release of the application.
- **Trigger:** Manual, from the production deploy
- **Pulls from branch:** production
- **Executes:** pipeline/deploy/production-flip
- **Success push branch:** n/a
- **On success:** nothing - you've reached the end of the pipeline!

The pipeline and your team

Even with an automated pipeline, it's important to focus on communication with your team throughout the development of features. You're more than likely using a chat application, so setting up integrations with your pipeline to notify users when a new build has passed or failed is a great aid.

Before deploying between your various environments, it's always a good idea to check in with the team to see if that's ok. For example, if you have clients using your staging environment to preview changes before they go to production, you might want to check these on the continuous environment before deploying. While you may be happy with your own work, your colleagues may need more time to check over theirs.

Most pipeline tools have good visibility on what changes triggered certain builds and, with manual steps, who triggered the build. This isn't to associate blame in the event something goes wrong, but it brings ownership to a deploy by having this visibility.

Variations

Even though the example we've used in this chapter is linear, not all pipelines need to be. A pipeline step could trigger multiple other steps allowing for different tasks to run in parallel. Unit tests, code standard checks and performance metrics are all things that could be run independently of one another.

The benefit of running tasks in parallel is that you get a reduced feedback loop, the time it takes to know whether a pipeline build can continue or whether it fails. The faster you're aware of a failing build, the faster a resolution can be made.

Other variations to pipelines could include post-deploy tasks that run smoke tests on a deploy to ensure it was successful, or to run security checks. These would save you having to spend time doing this manually, and would let you know sooner when things aren't as they should be.

Improvements to your pipeline

As we'll discuss in Chapter 10, it's important to always look for ways to improve your workflow; don't let your pipeline remain static and fixed once it has been setup. For every manual step in your pipeline, lookout for automated solutions that will ultimately save you hours throughout the life of your project.

Chapter 6: Keeping Quality High

by Richard Foster

One of the primary motivations to practice Continuous Delivery is that it helps facilitate the delivery of higher quality code.

In this chapter we'll discuss some techniques, tools and best practices you can employ to keep your pipelines moving, and how you can compel developers to push quality code often by rewarding them for attention to detail, while not punishing them for making mistakes.

One change at a time

Typically, the development process means making a change and testing it, then making another and testing again. Employing this technique of incremental development allows complex features to form in a timely, precise fashion, and is rewarded in many areas of software development.

Breaking large changesets down into smaller, self contained commits means they're much more readable and easily understood, with the added benefit that shared understanding of a project doesn't get lost in a slew of massive isolated updates.

Small changes are easy to store in your head and thinking of ways to improve them is simple. If others can easily understand your changes, they are more likely to make suggestions on ways to improve your code. If they can't, they'll leave it and assume it just works.

Keeping it together with tests

You've made a change in one part of your application to fix a bug, and it's caused a bug somewhere else to spring up. Maybe an old bug you thought you'd squashed, or something entirely new.

You've probably experienced this before, as it's a fairly common occurrence when developing complex applications, and can unfortunately be easily missed.

Without a robust test suite which includes unit tests to ensure your business logic is sound, as well as feature tests to ensure the user can actually use every part of it, mistakes like these can easily be missed, and buggy code can leak out to production.

Testing should come early and often, both locally and, as mentioned in the previous chapter, in the first step of your build pipeline. Coupled with small commits, a good test suite, run regularly, means problems are discovered very quickly.

Run less often, you would eventually find yourself in a position of needing to pore over tens, possibly hundreds, of commits to find the root of the problem.

If every commit to master is tested, then bugs introduced in a commit of a few lines can be found quickly. Better yet, fixing them so early is cheaper in terms of development time, than it is when the feature has reached production, and quicker fixes means more time for the fun parts of software development.

Testing so frequently has its consequences, however. Test suites are slow. As projects grow, you can see your test step grow from seconds, to minutes, even to hours on very large projects, which is clearly a frustrating impediment to shipping continuously. You want the time between development and production to be as short as possible.

Unfortunately, there is no definitive fix for this, for many it is what it is. Some developers, however, advocate only testing new code and crucial areas of your codebase in build steps, such as the checkout process of an e-commerce store, for example. This means bugs can still appear and get missed, but it also dramatically reduces the amount of code which needs to be tested, speeding up your build step and reducing your time to production.

Frequently pushing to your central repository can alleviate some of the pain of all this. You can push code and continue working, and only stop when you notice the build failing. The tests can just run in the background, frequently enough to alert you when something goes wrong, but not demanding so much of your attention that you can't get other work done asynchronously.

Stay beautiful

The easiest projects you've ever worked on are the projects which had consistent, readable code. Any developer can move faster by writing ugly code that works, but as soon as somebody else comes along the work suffers. Their pace slows as they come to grips with it. Finding a bug, or the right places to implement something new, becomes much more time consuming.

Maintaining readability of a codebase is paramount because projects which are easily understood are easy to work on. An app's source code is a manual for future developers, the code you write will become the standard you and others will follow when working on that project - and even future projects - so it behooves you to follow best practices at all times.

If we use automated tools to codify conventions we like, and test every revision of a project against them, sloppy work is more difficult to get through the pipeline. There are a number of tools that can be run on every build step of your deployment pipeline to ensure the code passing through is of a high quality.

For example, as one of the first steps of a Ruby project's build step, we run Tailor and Cane, which are static analysis tools that review the style of every Ruby file in the codebase against a set of rules we define.

Tailor checks the cosmetics, such as whether the whitespace is correct, or whether all method names are in lower snakecase. It checks that the code in our project matches our own guidelines.

Cane checks the complexity of code by, as an example, using an ABC metric to analyse how much a single method is trying to achieve, so that we can ensure the methods we're writing make sense and follow DRY conventions.

In Javascript we use ESLint, a newcomer to the linting world. Like Tailor, it checks our Javascript code against defined rules, and supports languages which transpile to Javascript, such as React's JSX syntax.

Fixing these syntax issues and accidental complexities as they come up is really helpful. Even if you're just pushing a small fix which is a few lines long, ignoring the quality of that code to speed up development would allow the quality of your codebase as a whole to suffer.

Preventing bad code from entering production forces the codebase to maintain a good shape, and although this may slow developers down in the short term, it improves productivity in the long term.

Brakeman, a Ruby 'vulnerability scanner', is another tool you can add to your static analysis arsenal. It can be used in builds to check for potential exploits your applications may be open to, so they can be cut off before reaching production. Although any tool which relies solely on static analysis and generic assumptions can't catch every possible point of attack, knowing that we're safe from common or simple exploits after a short build time is good for peace of mind.

Fail like a pro

Fixing problems quickly as they come up actually speeds up development as a whole and ultimately encourages developers to get it right the first time, to take their time in developing new features and make sure they're as good as they can be when they're pushed.

By developing with this framework around your deployment process, there is little fear of accidentally pushing code which could harm a customer's experience, the experience of future developers, or our own experience working on a codebase. Code which isn't good enough gets rejected, and you fix it.

Be happy

Ultimately, many of these tools and use cases focus on ways to get developers working well together, following agreed best practices and conventions, taking time on their work and continuously receiving feedback on what they've achieved. This attention to detail makes us proud of our work, and encourages developers to shepherd their changes to production, rather than throwing them in the wind.

Giving responsibility to developers makes them care about the quality of the code. They care about helping the customer, they want to see it being used and appreciated. Furthermore, by deploying regularly while keeping quality high, any small fixes needed once a feature hits production can be picked up by the developer best suited for the job.

Tests, QA, feedback and linters all, at first glance, slow development down, but in the long run, they provide a safety net for creativity and experimentation, which results in better, more stable code and happier developers and customers.

Chapter 7: Feature Toggles

by Rory MacDonald

When practising Continuous Delivery, it's important that your application is deployable at all times. This can introduce some challenges, especially when you have features that span multiple builds, or bug fixes that need to get into production quickly.

In this chapter, we're going to look at some of the techniques that we use to keep our applications deployable. We'll look at why branches (particularly long-lived ones) can be the kiss-of-death, why techniques like feature toggles are useful, but should be used with caution, and why you should focus on actually delivering small incremental changes to production.

Decoupling deployment and release

We've all run into this problem before: you've got a set of changes that have been in development for weeks. For whatever reason, they cannot be deployed through to production. Suddenly there is a small but urgent bug fix that needs to be deployed right away. What do you do?

By using feature toggles and enabling or disabling features, you could disable the offending feature in production and deploy your bug fix through your pipeline. However, without a toggle, you're probably going to need to revert your code to an earlier state, implement the bug fix and then deploy this through your pipeline, before re-applying the bug fix to master. This is risky, potentially complex, and the sort of thing you really should be trying to avoid.

Prevent long-lived branches

Some people would advocate developing the feature in its own branch and merging this back into master once the feature is complete. This creates an additional set of challenges and goes against many of the principles of continuous integration (where you should be integrating into a master branch multiple times per day).

Implementing Feature Toggles

The basic idea behind feature toggles is that you have a configuration system that allows you to toggle features on or off depending on some factors, such as environment, user profile or market. The running application then uses these toggles to decide whether or not to show the feature.

The actual implementation can take many forms. At its simplest, you will have a static configuration file within your application, which you deploy to production for the toggled changes to take effect. Some teams use more complex feature toggling systems, to allow runtime feature toggling via web interfaces or for toggling features within a canary build or quality assurance environment.

There are obviously a number of benefits to feature toggles, such as the ability to gradually roll out new features to users, proper decoupling of the deployment and release of code, and obviously the huge benefits around keeping your continuous delivery process working.

Branching in code vs. branching in source control

One of the biggest criticisms of feature toggles is that they can introduce unnecessary code branching into your application. You are effectively moving the branches a level down, out of version control and into your application, and you're putting features into conditionals, which increases the cyclomatic complexity of your application.

This code branching needs to be managed or you are fairly quickly going to start accruing technical debt. As a general rule, the quicker you can remove a feature toggle, the better. Toggles should be a short-term solution and not code that remains within your application for years to come.

Added test complexity

Another area in which you need to consider the impact of feature toggles, is within your test suite. There is a significant overhead to testing all toggle combinations, and frankly, it can be difficult to justify the impact this has on your test suite performance. Martin Fowler recommends having tests that cover:

- All the toggles that are expected to be on in the next release
- All toggles on

We believe this is a sensible default, but it is also important that you consider the best approach for your application. If you are dealing in high-stakes software, then it may be worth accepting this performance hit.

Small incremental releases

Feature toggles are great but, before introducing them, you should first try and break features down into small, incremental and releasable chunks. By doing this, you're minimising risk and more quickly realising value from your development effort.

As a developer, it's your responsibility to manage application complexity. Try to adopt a 'small and incremental' mindset as your default course-of-action, as this has the lowest complexity overhead.

Only when this becomes impossible to achieve should you look towards feature toggles (or any other technique), as they add complexity and ideally you want to minimise this as much as possible.

Chapter 8: Keeping a Clear Path to Production

by Luke Morton

In order to enjoy the benefits of Continuous Delivery it is imperative to be able to deploy all the way to production at any time. Anything that prevents a deploy to production is a blocker, and keeping that pathway clear is the hardest part of implementing and maintaining a continuous delivery of software.

Broken builds

The first step of a Continuous Delivery pipeline is the build step. A typical build step will run your tests, check the style of your code, point out overly complex methods and more. This means your build step has a lot of ways to fail. This is A Good Thing because it catches issues early, but it also means it's a prime candidate for blocker status.

The solution to broken builds is obvious: fix them and fix them fast. The rule in our team is that you must own your build failure. As soon as the build breaks, let your colleagues know that you are looking into it. You drop whatever you are doing and try to fix it immediately. If you cannot fix the problem quickly you back your changes out with a git revert, or something similar.

Preventive measures can be taken to reduce the likelihood of broken builds, such as your developers running the build script locally.

Parity between environments is also important. Running your tests locally and seeing them pass to then see them fail when they run on the build server is never fun. For example, bugs can arise by using different databases in different environments. Where possible use the same database management system everywhere. Same goes for asset storage, if you use Amazon S3 for file storage in production you're better off using it in every other environment too.

On flickering builds

Flickering tests are those which sometimes pass and sometimes fail. Often, the cause will be a test that sets up state and does not clear it afterwards, therefore affecting the result of a subsequent test run.

Another cause we've found are tests that run in headless browsers such as Selenium and PhantomJS. Sometimes expectations on page content will fail because an asynchronous request has not completed yet and therefore hasn't changed the page content as expected yet.

The nature of flickering tests is corrosive to Continuous Delivery discipline. You will often find engineers just rerun tests several times in the hope they will pass, which obviously affects the clear path to production. Also, if your build could fail at any time, and if your build time is upwards of more than a few minutes, a flickering test can really slow you down.

The cure to flickering tests is to either resolve their flickering nature as soon as you notice them or delete them. Removing the test is better than having it flicker and demotivate your engineers.

Work In Progress

Engineers practicing Continuous Delivery should push early and often. This means committing small chunks of work and pushing them to your application's master branch several times an hour.

The problem with your engineers pushing code is that the tests may pass but the feature is not necessarily complete enough to be released to users. Incomplete work in your master branch that would affect a user is a blocker.

The dark launching of code is one way to circumvent this. Dark launching simply means the code is able to be deployed out to production but it is never accessed by users. The simplest way to dark launch a new feature is to release it under a new URL and not link to the URL from anywhere, which might seem crude, but is effective.

Feature toggles, which we covered in the previous chapter, are a more advanced way of dark launching. Simply wrap up your feature in a toggle and ensure it is disabled in production. We tend to use feature toggles if a feature is a change to an existing feature or is provided by a URL already accessible to users.

Unreviewed work

We have found that sometimes features can sit complete on staging, undeployable to production since the feature requires verification from a Customer, Product Owner or a colleague that simply hasn't had time . The external dependency on a Customer can really block your pipeline.

If you have limited reviews by Customers before deployment to production you are in luck. In these situations we encourage engineers to not move onto another task until the one they have just completed is reviewed. In fact we consider it incomplete until it's reviewed and deployed to production. This often forces the engineer to get up and get a colleague to immediately review their work.

If the feature must be checked by a Customer then the solution is more nuanced. We try to send features over to clients via instant messaging as soon as they are ready to be reviewed. This is similar to our internal approach above. Failing that, if we need to deploy a hotfix to production we will back the changes out with git revert and deploy our changes up. This is nasty, we know, but it often encourages you to change your policy of review or open up better lines of communication with your clients.

Dependency on other releases

From time to time we work with other teams to deliver software. We try to integrate into a single team where possible, to work from the same codebase. However we have dealt with situations where the other team is delivering an API that our team will have to interact with. Often we know the spec of the API before it is built so we can mock it out. Problems arise when a change to an API occurs and we update our code, but the API side has not implemented the change yet. A deployment to production would mean miscommunication with the API. This is a blocker.

Another variation of this is migrations not being run at the same time of deployment. If you push your code and it tries to interact with fields that do not exist yet, you're going to have a bad time. Another blocker.

The first solution we jump to is hacking the setup. We try and get their team to deliver the API in the same sprint and codebase as us, so we can't deploy them separately. This way we can always keep in sync. We would always recommend running migrations on deployment and not having a siloed DBA run them instead. You can often convince the Ops Person or DBA to allow you to run migrations if you promise to only commit non-destructive migrations, or get them to lock down DB permissions so you cannot drop tables, remove columns, etc.

Alternatively, if we cannot deliver as a single team, we get smart. Getting smart means using if statements. If this API call fails, fallback to using the older API call. If this field doesn't exist in the database, don't render it. This can get messy and should be cleaned up as soon as you can but it does unblock you.

Success of your Continuous Delivery practice depends on your ability to react and unblock your pipeline whenever issues arise. Broken builds occur and that's okay; your team needs to be drilled to respond and fix them as soon as possible. Work in progress and work ready for review is part of the software delivery process, but must be dealt with sensibly. Dependency on other releases should be avoided where possible but you can get smart too. Ultimately, if you develop a culture of responsibility for keeping the pathway clear, then you will truly start to benefit from Continuous Delivery.

Chapter 9: Challenges In Adopting Continuous Delivery

by Nick Wood

Adopting Continuous Delivery for a single team is tough, adopting it across a whole organisation exponentially more so. It's hard to catalogue all the issues a business may face during the transition, but in this chapter we'll discuss the common pitfalls.

Giving teams ownership

In a traditional software setup, with separate teams (product, architecture, development, QA, Ops, to name a few) a move to Continuous Delivery is likely impossible unless you have exceptional levels of communication between all teams. When each team is only responsible for their own output, without strong discipline it's hard to stave off a culture of throwing things over the wall, to the next team in line.

You feature pipeline might look something like this - it's ominously Waterfall:

```
[Product Team] => [Architecture] => [Software devlopment] => [QA] => [Ops]
```

On close inspection it's apparent that this pipeline isn't very fault tolerant. A failure in any single team prevents anyone else from doing their job! The other challenge is how to ensure that each of the five teams are working at the exact same rate.

If the Product Team are defining features faster than they can be architected, then we have a bottleneck. Items are sitting idle in the Architecture queue, waiting for someone to pick them up. Over time this leads to a massive Architecture backlog which becomes impossible to prioritise, and business goals may have changed by the time Architecture get around to tackling them.

The opposite problem is equally likely, and is probably happening simultaneously elsewhere in your process. Let's imagine the development team can build features faster than the architects can specify them, and also faster than QA can test them. There's now a very real chance that your developers will run out of stuff to do, so those bums on seats are costing you money and you're getting no return on that investment.

This is not to say that Architecture is always the problem, in practice your bottleneck could be anywhere.

In the example described above your pipeline looks like this, with the width of the pipe indicating the rate of work:

In such a system the flow of the whole is ultimately determined by the flow of the slowest team. Any team capacity above this is essentially wasted. As a stop gap you could expand your slower team to improve throughput, but ultimately all you will do is move the bottleneck elsewhere.

Bottlenecks are a disfunction and they'll lead to frustration of the team, and a culture of blaming others when they inevitably slow the system down. Fixing the problem needs a complete rework of the plumbing. Rather than each team being responsible for their part of the pipe, the team as a whole need to be responsible for the entire throughput of the system, this can only happen when the team is equally responsible for the whole:

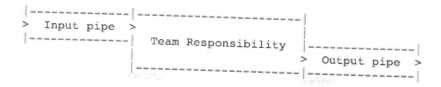

```
> Input pipe  >
                 Team Responsibility

                                     > Output pipe >
```

Any team, regardless of scope, will have its inputs and outputs; the adoption of Continuous Delivery is fundamentally about teaching teams to group up and share their dependencies, rather than being co-dependent on each other. Such a transformation won't happen overnight though.

Adopting this change in thinking can usually be accomplished in several discrete steps. You might start for example by joining the Dev & Test functions, by having testers and developers work closely with Architecture to define technical requirements. Testers can then write their tests whilst the developers write their code, and as they are both working on the same thing it's much easier for them to talk through issues to reach a common understanding.

The team should also share ownership of their output stream, ensuring that nothing goes to the Ops team until developers and testers alike are both happy. No more arguments along the lines of "testing should have caught the bug!" - the team either succeed together, or fail together.

Ensuring everyone is utilised effectively will likely require some element of cross skilling, ensuring that your devs know how to test code, and testers understand the system architecture; valuable side effects of the transition. That's not to say that there's no room for specialisation though - our goal isn't to have everyone equally skilled in all areas, just to ensure that everyone understands and is responsible for how the whole team works.

Measuring success

A key difficulty with Continuous Delivery, is changing how to measure success/progress. Many Agile methodologies start to fall down when faced with genuine Continuous Delivery. Take Scrum as one example, what value does a Sprint Demo have in such an environment?

In a two week sprint we'll have close to a dozen features in production by the end, so is there value sitting stakeholders down and running through features they've likely already seen? How does measuring a team's velocity over two weeks help us figure out where bottlenecks are so that we can improve? It's likely in such an environment that average cycle time, i.e. how long it takes to go from inception to production, will be a much more meaningful metric.

Delivering value to customers is the ultimate goal of any software project, though actually measuring this is generally quite difficult with a large change set. Once you are delivering atomic units of value in a Continuous Delivery fashion, it becomes much easier to measure this. By tracking key performance metrics from build to build you can easily see which builds had the biggest impact on value (conversion rate, or average session time being two common examples). Combine this with cycle time and you have two very powerful tools for determining the most valuable work for the team to focus on next.

Managing technical debt

It's relatively uncommon for the concepts of technical debt and code health/quality to be well understood outside of your immediate tech team, which is a shame, as these have a massive impact on your teams ability to perform or, as we defined it above, cycle time.

Exposing these metrics as loudly as you can is a great way to encourage the business to take more of an interest in them, and to prioritise improving them. It's much easier to make the business care about these metrics when faced with concrete data such as: "We spent a week on increasing test coverage in this section of our application by 50%, and sped up build times by 15% - this has removed a day from our mean cycle time for this component meaning we can get new features in front of customers 10-20% faster."

The reverse is also true: "Test coverage has dropped this month 20% and as a result we've seen more build failures and an increased cycle time" is a great way to make financially incentivised people care about your code health, and give teams space to take remedial action.

That's not to say our aim is to remove technical debt completely; consider treating technical debt like a financial one. Having lots of debt is probably a bad thing, but if you have a good rate of interest, debt becomes manageable, and in some cases even desired (lots of companies run at a deficit, and most homeowners have a mortgage for example). Paying off the entire debt in one go is probably not practical, but in order to get the debt under control it's important to keep up with interest (make sure you are not making your technical debt worse) and make regular down payments (take active steps towards improving the state of your codebase).

Technical debt is hard to measure, but using the metaphor above it can be understood by imagining our interest as a tax on every release. The more releases we do, the more important it is to keep this under control.

Helping customers embrace change

Arguably the hardest relationship to maintain as a software company is the one with your most important resource: your customers. They can also be one of the biggest challenges to Continuous Delivery. Changing your application frequently has both the ability to empower or frustrate your entire user base. As with many things, the devil is in the details.

Unless you're working in the rarified sector of delivering software to other developers, then it's highly likely that your customers don't understand how software is made at anything more than a superficial level. The first question you must ask yourself when adopting CD is "can our users handle a constantly evolving product?". If the answer to this question is 'no' then it's possible that Continuous Delivery is not for you.

An alternative approach might be to split your product into different 'release streams', such as a stable branch for customers who don't want change, and an alpha/beta channel for those who embrace it. This in some sense gives you the best of both worlds, as you can readily get feedback from your alpha channel customers. They feel like they are being listened to, and have a very real impact on shaping the product which they use.

Multiple release channels do add an overhead to every release, however, so this approach should be used with caution. It also probably wouldn't strictly be defined as

Continuous Delivery, but if it's your only barrier to Continuous Delivery then you might consider it worthwhile.

Continuous Delivery has a multitude of downsides if done poorly, but it also has tremendous potential upside if done well.

Chapter 10: The Future of Continuous Delivery

by Fareed Dudhia

We've discussed what Continuous Delivery is, the benefits, how to prepare your team for it, the challenges you may face adopting it, the tools you can use, how to build your pipeline and what you can do to make sure quality remains high, but how do you stay on top of the advances in Continuous Delivery?

At Made Tech, we're always trying to improve. We continuously question our own processes and implement (or remove) processes to eliminate pain points. This isn't about using the newest tech you read about on Hacker News. It's about letting people do their jobs better in order to deliver software faster. So, how do we continuously improve?

Retrospectives

Sprint retrospectives are an important part of not only a project lifecycle, but also how we continue to improve and iterate on our processes. After every sprint, we sit down with the product owner and our Scrum Master for about half an hour and look back over the sprint.

What went well? What went badly? How could we improve? Our scrum master comes up with novel ways for people involved in the project to vent about pain points in the previous sprint in a constructive, solution-orientated atmosphere. Each retrospective ends with a list of actionable ways to improve, and if previous improvements from earlier retrospectives were found to be particularly helpful, these can be rolled to other project teams.

Retrospectives are a great way to find processes that end up doing more harm than good, too. As with everything, it's about finding a balance between structuring a team member's output to maximise efficiency, while also making sure the processes aren't getting in the way of delivery. It's only by spending time sitting down and talking about what's working and what isn't that we can continue to improve delivery.

Dojos, Katas, Mobs and Talks

It's important that your developers continuously improve, too. After a certain amount of time working on a project, even the best developers have a tendency to settle into their own ways of doing things. Some developers can also be resistant to change. In order to improve going into the future, it's important to make sure that developers are all on the same page in regards to best practices, techniques, and maybe even languages and frameworks.

It's also important to get the most out of your developers. People who develop software for a living often have a lot of things to bring to the table outside of their project work. Looking into the future, talking about and honestly evaluating new technologies as they mature is an important part of staying afloat in the quickly moving technical world.

So what do we do about this? Every Friday, everyone who can spare the time is encouraged to join one of our group programming sessions. These are always organised organically, by people who want to talk about something with the team. These are usually organised loosely into one of the following categories:

Code Katas

A Code Kata is simply a programming exercise wherein a problem is taken, solved, and iterated over until it is of production standard. We usually use TDD to solve these problems. Everyone in the group has a chance to provide input. The goal of the exercise is to get everyone on the same page, programming-wise.

Code Katas are a big help for onboarding and demonstrating the standard of programming required at the company. No-one writes bad code when there's other people watching, especially when the problem is designed to encourage good programming practices.

Code Dojos

Our Code Dojos are usually long-running projects which are completed over a series of weeks. We divide an hour up roughly into chunks depending on how many people are attending. The laptop is then passed around so each person has about 5 minutes to contribute to the project.

The goal is usually to get everyone on the same page in regards to how we deliver software. Contributors are forced to commit early and often, lest their chunk of time go to waste. A good Code Dojo shows how quickly a project can take form without a long planning period, and helps developers get over their fear of uncertainty.

Mob Programming

A Mob Programming exercise is similar to a Code Dojo, but it's with everyone around the same laptop, making cases for their ideas and then implementing them. Everyone is around one laptop, so the team is forced to work together, building on each others ideas. We often use Mob Programming as a way to refactor some of our existing code.

Talks and interactive demonstrations

One of the most valuable things that our developers do is give talks and interactive demonstrations on new techniques or technologies they think we should be using. Our modern npm-based javascript stack was introduced to us by one of our more recent hires by a talk he gave on a Friday. He made a strong enough case that we should be using better javascript in production, and now we are. We recently deployed our first projects in React, which was introduced to the team at a similar talk.

Talks and demonstrations give the team a chance to air concerns about new technologies. We can decide if they're right for us. Gentle introductions to new techniques and technologies can help to ease any resistance that team members might feel. In our opinion, organically improving beats company-mandated improvement, hands down.

Thirty Thursdays

So how do we find time to eliminate pain points? Where do we get the time to try out new ideas? If our sprint retrospectives bring up pains in process, when can we research tools that might help us, or develop our own?

The answer, for us, are 'Thirty Thursdays'[12]. Our developers, barring emergencies that need immediate attention, have Thursdays to develop ideas of their own choosing outside of project work. Usually there's a Thirty Thursday pitch meeting, where people pitch their ideas and recruit other team members to help them. We've used the time to produce learning materials, canary builds, implement automated visual regression testing, and even make what you're reading right now.

State of the Art

New technology is always a big part of looking to the future. Technologies are increasingly born, hyped, and killed in ever-quicker cycles. It's often difficult to keep up with what the "state of the art" actually is.

The best technologies still stand the test of time, but often the level of corporate hype around certain companies' offerings can make it difficult to distinguish the soon-to-be-replaced tools from the tech that will stand the test of time. We use a few techniques to figure out what technology is worth trying out and what is worth leaving.

Firstly, check the source code! Have a look (or have a developer look) and see what you're using actually is. See how it works. See how easy it would be to fit into your existing workflow.

Secondly, are your favourite high-profile developers talking about it? Are they excited about it? Most importantly, are they using it in production? Has anyone written about the use cases that the technology is best suited to, and are you sure that you aren't trying to shoehorn it into your workflow simply because it's the "hot new thing"?

Thirdly, check out Technology Radar. They publish a bi-annual list of techniques and technologies to adopt. They're very level-headed about new tech; they'll advise to "trial" certain technologies and reassess them as they mature. It's a great resource.

In conclusion, there's no foolproof method for ensuring that your company will adapt perfectly in this ever-changing industry. Hopefully the ideas outlined here will have given you some ideas, but ultimately every company works best in its own culture, and the points above are best treated as ideas to help inspire techniques that could prove useful to your company in their own way. In other words, Your Mileage May Vary.

That said, we believe that the general concepts we've outlined should stand the test of time. We're very proud of what we do here at Made Tech, and we believe strongly in our culture. A big part of our culture is about sharing what we believe makes us effective, and this book has been the biggest example of this principle so far. Of course, delivering quality software is a business with innumerable facets, but we hope you have found it valuable.

Thank you.

---

12 The name 'Thirty Thursday' comes from a fleeting moment of terrible maths. Somewhere along the way, it was declared that one day out of a five day working week is equivalent to thirty percent of a working week, and, more importantly, 'Twenty Thursday' doesn't roll off the tongue nearly so well.

About Made Tech

Founded in 2010 and based in London, we're a team who deliver software using what we consider to be modern best practices, with techniques such as agile, cloud automation, continuous integration, domain-driven design, lean software development and test-driven development.

We favour modern technology stacks such as Ruby on Rails, Django, NodeJS and GoLang over their legacy alternatives, all of which enable us to deliver value to our customers quicker.

Find us at www.madetech.com

Made in the USA
Lexington, KY
24 June 2018